W9-AMP-313

Let's Find Ads on Clothing

by Mari Schuh

first step nonfiction

Lerner Publications ◆ Minneapolis

The images in this book are used with the permission of: © Blue Jean Images/Alamy, p. 4; © Frances Roberts/Alamy, pp. 5, 19, 21; © medeni/Alamy, p. 6; © Kathy deWitt/Alamy, p. 7; © iStockphoto.com/GlobalStock, p. 8; AP Photo/Sean D Elliot, p. 9; © Michael S. Williamson/The Washington Post via Getty Images, p. 10; © Colin Underhill/Alamy, p. 11; © Image Source Plus/Alamy, p. 12; Greg Thompson/Icon Sportswire via AP Images, p. 13; AP Photo/The Daily Gazette, Marc Schultz, p. 14; © Barbara Haddock Taylor/TNS/ZUMAPRESS.com, p. 15; © Donald Bowers/Stringer/Getty Images, pp. 16, 22; © Jamie Squire/Getty Images, p. 17; © Hill Street Studios/Blend/Getty Images, p. 18; © Ute Grabowsky/Photothek/Getty Images, p. 20.
Cover: © Frances Roberts/Alamy.

Main body text set in ITC Avant Garde Gothic Std Medium 21/25.
Typeface provided by International Typeface Corp.

Lerner Publications Company
A division of Lerner Publishing Group, Inc.
241 First Avenue North
Minneapolis, MN 55401 USA

For reading levels and more information, look up this title at www.lernerbooks.com.

Library of Congress Cataloging-in-Publication Data

Schuh, Mari C., 1975–
    Let's find ads on clothing / by Mari Schuh.
        pages cm. — (First step nonfiction : learn about advertising)
    Includes index.
    ISBN 978-1-4677-9469-5 (lb : alk. paper) — ISBN 978-1-4677-9655-2 (pb : alk. paper) — ISBN 978-1-4677-9656-9 (eb pdf)
    1. Advertising—Clothing and dress—Juvenile literature. 2. Advertising—Juvenile literature.
I. Title.
    HF6161.C44S38 2016
    659.19'687—dc23   5857   2015015203

Manufactured in the United States of America
1 – CG – 12/31/15

Table of Contents

Companies and Ads

Companies want people to buy **products**.

A shirt is a product.

Clothing is a product.

Ad is short for advertisement.

Companies pay for **ads**. The ads tell people about products.

6

Ads can make people want
to buy products.

Ads are on TV and on
signs. Ads are on the
8 Internet.

Ads on Clothing

Ads are on clothing too.

Clothing ads tell people about **brands** and companies.

Some shoes have logos.

Logos on clothing are ads. Brand names are ads.

Brand names can be on
jeans.

Ads can be on T-shirts.
Hats can show ads as well.

How Ads Work

Ads ask people to buy or do things.

Some ads tell you about TV
shows or movies.

An ad can make
you want a toy.

Other ads show toys.

Ads can show sports teams.

Ads can make clothes seem
fun to wear.

Your friend might want a certain brand of jeans.

Ads can make someone want certain clothes.

Ads You Wear

What clothes do you like to wear?

Some of your clothes might
show ads.

What do the ads on your clothes tell people?

Glossary

ads – messages that try to sell products or services

brands – the names of certain products or companies

companies – groups that make or sell products or services

logos – symbols that stand for a company. A company's logo is often found on its products.

products – items that are made and sold

Index